RAISING READERS

RAISING READERS

PRACTICAL ADVICE

FROM A READING TEACHER AND MOM

MELANIE ESKILDSEN

This book is dedicated to my devoted and hardworking husband, Brian. He supports my adventurous ideas and loves me unconditionally.

To my beautiful three children, thank you for being curious and fun loving. You are my world.

My love of books and literature is deeply rooted by Grandma June. She brought books into my life and encouraged me to be a lifelong reader and learner.

AUTHOR'S NOTE

I'M EXCITED THIS BOOK IS IN YOUR HANDS! You are a parent or caregiver wanting to immerse their child in a love of reading. I am not a researcher or a professor. I am a mom of three and a reading teacher. This book is written with practical, hands-on ideas you can immediately try. My hope is you will find this book easy to read with activities you can implement the day you read it.

About fifteen years ago my principal told me I was moving to a reading teacher position. My first reaction was, um ok-now what!? I was hesitant but I quickly embraced teaching reading. I love introducing our children and my students to new stories, characters, and information. I absolutely adore watching students turn into fluent readers. To explain to a child with graphs how they are growing as a reader is exhilarating. Over the years students have introduced me to new authors and new characters. And now as our children are entering young adulthood, I reflect back on all the teachable reading moments we shared with fondness.

Today we are raising our family in central Wisconsin where the winters are long and the commute is short. The advice shared with you in this book comes from my experience as a mom, kindergarten teacher, private tutor, and a reading teacher for ages five to eighteen. While I understand every child is different and every family is different, I'm excited you want to raise your child to develop a love of reading!

—MELANIE ESKILDSEN

CONTENTS

Chapter 4: Experiences to Build Background Knowledge

Chapter 5: Keep it Going!

CHAPTER 1

RAISING READERS—LET'S GET STARTED!

First, I'd like to introduce you to Charlie. I was asked to test Charlie at the beginning of second grade. His teacher had some concerns about his reading skills. He lacked confidence and motivation to read, and seemed to be behind the other students. So, I went through the battery of tests I give students when classroom teachers have concerns. I work as a reading teacher in central Wisconsin. My sole job is to assess reading skills and then help students become proficient readers and writers. Now back to Charlie, he started in one of my classes. We began working together daily to improve his reading skills. Slowly that smile that laughed at my silly jokes was now smiling about books. He completed his reading homework and asked for more. His classroom performance was quickly improving. His teacher noticed. His parents noticed. And I noticed. One day I asked him a simple question, "What did I do to help you be able to read?" His response brought tears to my eyes and joy to my heart. He simply said, "You give me books I can read."

Was it really this simple? Maybe not for some kids, but for Charlie, yes it really was that easy. I was the first adult in his life to really tune in to his reading needs. I helped him find books that he could read and enjoy. We played games with words, and we practiced story comprehension. All these things helped him to become a lover of reading. Charlie was dismissed from my class about six months after he started. Occasionally I run into his mom at the grocery store. She always reports Charlie is doing well and is still in love with reading.

Throughout the book you will read about more kids like Charlie and my own children. In our home and in my classroom, I have found simple and practical ways to raise children who love reading. The proof is in the three children we have raised and the countless students that have entered my classroom. My simple belief: embrace everyday life as a teachable moment. Over time, those moments culminate into children who love learning, reading, and writing.

If you are expecting a book with the latest research on the newest and greatest reading techniques, this is not the book. Nope no boring research to read. There will be no charts or percentages. You will not be reading about the latest and "greatest" fad in reading. This book shares real experiences as a teacher and mom. My hope is by the end of the book you will be encouraged to raise your own reader.

You may be wondering about my credentials. First, I am a mom. Some may describe me as a fierce mama bear. Our children are our world. They are my sunshine on cloudy days and my inspiration on difficult days. The day we attended our first funeral as a family I knew we had raised some amazing children in many ways. Our children were all under the age of six. My uncle passed away from a quick battle with cancer. Even though our children did not know my uncle well, we loaded up the minivan and started out on our three-hour drive to northern Wisconsin. Conversations in the car revolved around funeral procedures, customs, and ways to remember loved ones. We seized the moment to teach them and front load information before we got to the funeral. Therefore, this experience gave them new vocabulary, new experiences, and new knowledge. We purposely used an everyday life experience to make it a teachable moment.

Uncle Charles was an avid Harley Davidson rider. When we arrived at the church we were overwhelmed with the number of motorcycles and riders that had come to celebrate his life. And it was just that, a celebration of his life where mourners had an opportunity to share their favorite memories. It was at the beginning of the service when this mama was overcome with emotions. Our youngest daughter climbed up into my lap while the other two kids held my hand. Brian leaned in and whispered: *the code word is pineapple.* Whenever you need someone to hold your hand or hug you, say "pineapple." His idea made all of us crack a small smile. That moment brought us closer together as a family creating a bond where children are nurtured and loved. It is this strong family bond that has helped us to raise three incredible kids who love reading and learning.

Second, I am a wife to a husband who supports all my wild ideas. Writing this book was one of those ideas! Brian and I met before my senior year in college. We dated for what seemed like forever before tying the knot. To this day he claims he never proposed, it was the dog's fault. Our dog, Maggie, delivered the engagement ring to me in her mouth. Together we love going on adventures. From hiking to snowmobiling and everything in between. We are a pretty amazing team that cooperates and always does what is best for our children.

And third, I am a reading teacher. I have a Bachelor of Science degree in Early Childhood Education with an additional reading teacher license. Straight out of college I taught kindergarten for five years. I took a break from the classroom to be a full-time mama. When I went back to work, I taught kindergarten for a year and then was moved to a reading teacher position. I was hesitant at first. Teaching one single subject was new to me. Plus, my principal was adding middle school students to my caseload. It did not take long to fall deeply in love with teaching children, of any age, to read and write proficiently. As a reading teacher I assess students' reading skills. If they are reading significantly below grade level, they are placed in my class. Together we work in small groups instructing them on the reading skills they are lacking. Whether they are young or old, the classroom routine is similar.

As they enter my room, we spend a few minutes checking in with each other. They tell me about frustrations, successes, and sometimes a book they have been reading. I give them my full attention as they talk, which validates their story and their importance to me. This check in time builds our relationship which lends itself to a genuine learning environment.

Depending on what students need, we begin by either practicing sight words or manipulating letter sounds. Teachers call it phonics and phonemic awareness. We read a new book each day from our reading series. Most days younger students spend a few minutes rereading a book from the previous day. We often talk about how it is ok to read a book more than one time. Maybe the second or third time you will notice different words or something new in a picture. Next, I introduce the new book and characters. Taking the time to "get into" a new book is worthwhile. Children, and adult readers alike, can begin to predict the story and jump start their imagination. Whether it is a fiction or nonfiction book, taking time to introduce a book also gives students an opportunity to activate prior knowledge.

Just to clarify, fictional books tell stories about pretend events or lives. Nonfiction books are loaded with facts, real life events, information, and pictures. Prior knowledge is knowledge and experiences a reader brings to the book. For example, a child that has taken ballet lessons will be more familiar with words related to ballet than a student with zero ballet experience. We will get more into prior knowledge in chapter four.

After I introduce the book, I give students the opportunity to quietly read to themselves. Read that again and let that sink in for a minute. I allow students to read a new book quietly to themselves. Now part of this is asking them to read loud enough so I can hear them reading. Letting students read a book for the first time alone takes away the fear of reading in front of others. It also allows students time to independently practice reading and practice problem solving when reading unknown words.

Pause for a minute and think about all the processes happening as a child learns to read. They are figuring out letter to sound correspondence, or what sounds letters make. Or what sounds do all these letters make when I put them together. They are recalling sight words from memory. Children look at the pictures for enjoyment and to understand the story.

When everyone finishes reading, we discuss the book. Sometimes it is in the form of recall or retelling information. Other times it is talking about why a character behaved in a certain way. Or maybe think about what might happen after the story ends. Lastly, students write about their reading. They may be given a very vague or specific writing prompt depending on the age and book type. For students who are just learning to write, our writing practice is more modeled. We may craft a sentence together leaving them to fill in a blank.

What I have described above is how a typical reading lesson runs in my classroom. Not all days are exactly like this. What we do depends on what my students need. One day we may spend the entire class practicing sight words with modeling dough. Or practicing manipulating sounds in a word. For example, if you take off the letter c in cat and add an h, what is the new word? Some days we play letter sound bingo or a memory game. Changing what we do keeps kids interested, engaged, and constantly learning.

It may not surprise you that we have raised our children as if our home is a classroom. You will not only end up with children who love reading but children who love to learn and are curious.

WHAT A YOUNG READER LOOKS LIKE

Young readers are curious and sponge-like. They are ready to soak up all the information, skills, and experiences you give them. Every reader has unique skills and characteristics. While learning comes easy for some it may not for others. If you are concerned about your child's development, I suggest you talk with your pediatrician. They will be able to tell you about normal developmental milestones. A pediatrician will also be able to help you contact professionals to assess their developmental skill levels.

Back to what younger readers are like, most young readers are overflowing with curiosity. You will notice this when they ask you why things happen or how things work. I know it is tiring to answer the same questions over and over, but your child is gaining knowledge and vocabulary words. They are learning about the world around them. One day this information will help them as they read a book.

Young readers need you to teach them about the world of reading. I like to call it *book skills*. And just like riding a bike or playing football, children need to learn book skills before they are ready to read. Having basic book skills shows a child has a basic understanding of print and how it works.

Here is a list of what I look for when informally observing children on their book skills:

1. Are they holding the book the proper way?
2. Do they show knowledge that books move from left to right?
3. Do they show knowledge that the book goes from top to bottom?
4. Are they able to turn the pages of a book?

When the child shows knowledge of these book skills, they are starting to develop the skills needed to be a reader. If your child is struggling with these skills, try modeling. For example, say "I am holding the book like this, so the pictures and words are not upside down" or "When I start reading, I start here." Point at where to start reading and follow the print with your finger. Modeling, or showing your child what to do, will help them quickly learn how books work.

WHY RAISING A READER IS IMPORTANT

Since you are reading this book, I probably do not need to convince you too much that raising a reader is important. You picked up this book in the hopes it will help you raise a child who loves reading. Explaining the "why" is trickier than I thought it would be.

It has been so fun watching our children grow and learn to read. From making letters with clay to reading college textbooks. You are probably in the trenches with your young child. It is a busy time of life that's for sure. It may be difficult to see past the moment of time you are in. But trust me it's coming. The day they decide on their own to read for pleasure is near. Or high school graduation day when you watch them receive a diploma for twelve years of hard work. College graduations are now on our horizon, my how time flies!

REASONS WHY RAISING A READER IS IMPORTANT

1. Reading lets you experience different vocabulary.
2. Reading allows you to learn about any topic you desire.
3. Reading offers new ideas and/or new techniques on a topic.
4. Reading helps you learn about people and places.
5. Reading fiction lets you escape from the present.
6. When you are reading the right book, reading is a pleasure.

As I thought about why learning to read is important, I decided to ask students and my children what they thought. Here is what they had to say.

When I asked my students why it is important to read, they said:

> **2nd grader,** "Reading helps you to be able to learn. Like you can read to learn about something new."
>
> **2nd grader,** "If you don't know how to read you are not going to learn very much."
>
> **3rd grader,** "Once you get in higher grades you have to read a lot, a lot of books. You can't just guess at the words."

Out of our three children, the oldest, who enjoys reading the most, said it is hard to pinpoint exactly why reading is important, it just is. She also said it gives you independence, lets you learn new things, and opens up new possibilities.

HOW TO RAISE A READER

As I stated earlier, my belief: embrace everyday life as a teachable moment. Over time, those moments culminate into children who love learning, reading, and writing. Each and every day we have the opportunity to embrace teachable moments with young children. It is within those teachable moments where you are raising a reader. Taking the time to let a child help write a grocery list teaches organization and how to write a list. Spending time in the kitchen reading a recipe and creating something gives a purpose to reading. Writing a thank you card to a loved one for a gift teaches gratitude and writing for others to read.

WHAT IS TO COME

As you continue reading, we will explore the pitfalls and positives of technology. I will suggest some websites that my children and students find particularly engaging. Chapter 3 explores reading as a daily habit to encourage a love of reading.

Later I will share how experiences build background knowledge and how this knowledge is useful to reading. And finally, I will share how we continue to be excited about books and learning up to high school. As you read, I hope you will make use of the journal pages and smile at the pictures of our children. I would love for you to connect with me on social media or email and share pictures of your readers! **melanie.eskildsen.author@gmail.com**

I WANT TO REMEMBER:

_____

_____

_____

_____

_____

_____

_____

_____

MY CHILD ALREADY HAS SOME BOOK SKILLS:

_____

_____

_____

_____

_____

_____

_____

LEARNING TO READ IS IMPORTANT BECAUSE:

_____

_____

_____

_____

_____

_____

_____

CHAPTER 1

CHAPTER 2

TECHNOLOGY-UGH

If I am being honest, I am not an expert when it comes to technology. It does not scare me, nor do I avoid it. When I am tasked with learning something new, I pick it up quickly. However, I am a firm believer in not having kids on technology frequently.

When it comes to technology and children, where do you stand? Technology can be engaging and motivating for some children. In the other corner technology can be overused by children and parents. This overuse causes a lack of engagement with each other and with real life.

TECHNOLOGY AT OUR HOUSE

When I think of technology I am referring to television, video games, tablets, phones etc. While little to no technology worked well for our family, it may be different for you.

While reflecting on technology, I am realizing how very little our children had access to while growing up. I did not have a cell phone until they were in middle school. It never would have crossed my mind to put a phone in the hands of a two-year-old. Today it is more common. When we go to an appointment of any kind, I am that lone parent reading a book or better yet talking to my children, rather than tending to my phone.

When our children were growing up, they were limited to thirty minutes of television a day. On occasion we watched movies together. And when the kids were sick, technology rules went out the window. We allowed more television time to help ease the boredom of being sick and miserable. Our children did not have their own phone until eighth grade. This seemed to be the year they started being more involved at school. A phone helped them stay connected with us and their friends.

RULES FOR PHONES AT OUR HOUSE
1. Parents can look at it whenever they want
2. Ask permission before downloading any apps
3. No phones during a meal or holiday gathering
4. Phones get put away at 8:30pm for the night

Your phone is not a substitute for you. I am grateful I did not have a cell phone as I was raising our children. I often see young parents so engrossed in their phone they are missing out on teachable moments. They are missing out on sharing experiences with their child. Your young child loves your attention and sharing special moments with you. They may not be old enough to express that to you, but those moments are making an impact both big and small. For children to grow into proficient readers and writers they need words. They need a background of experiences to draw from when reading a new book. These things happen when you are face to face interacting with your child.

POSITIVES OF TECHNOLOGY

Technology does have benefits. Some games or educational websites can be very engaging for a child. The technology aspect may grab their attention in ways paper and pencil cannot. Some may argue technology improves a child's memory or fine motor skills.

Technology allows us quick and easy access to information. Have a question? Look it up quickly on your phone or computer. Need directions to somewhere new? Look it up on your phone.

Technology is everywhere from stores to theme parks. Even though I may not be partial to technology, it is a part of our world and here to stay.

NEGATIVES OF TECHNOLOGY

On the opposite side are the negative aspects of technology. Some would argue technology decreases the attention span of a child. Most content on the internet is not developmentally appropriate for young children. This can lead to misinformation because they are not able to discern fact from fiction.

Cyberbullying has also become an issue in our modern world. We all know it is easier to "say" things via text or email rather than face to face. Words can also be interpreted differently via text or email.

FAVORITE WEBSITES FOR YOUNG READERS

My list of favorite websites is short, mostly because when you find something you love why not stick with that? This list is far from exhaustive, so make sure and find what works for you and your young reader(s)!

https://www.starfall.com/h/

My all-time favorite website is Starfall.com. There is a free version and a paid version. I am honestly not sure of the difference between the two versions. I use the free version. In my classroom I use it when teaching letter identification and letter sounds. I use it to teach and practice vowel rules. The website is interactive, colorful, and child friendly.

https://www.readingrockets.org/

The Reading Rockets organization is dedicated to offering information and resources for teachers, parents, and caregivers about literacy. Literacy is the ability to read and write effectively to communicate with others. They offer a wide range of researched based articles and tips to help your child become a reader.

Several years ago, the Reading Rockets website sparked an idea in me. They offer reading adventure packs on their website. Reading adventure packs are theme based and literacy rich activities for families to complete at home. I printed these packs and created Reading Adventure Backpacks for families to check out and use at home. To date there are twenty-five Reading Adventure Backpacks available to anyone at our school. Each backpack contains three books, a theme-based packet of activities, a journal to document the families' experiences, and a reading buddy toy. Reach out to me if you want help starting your own Reading Adventure Backpack program!

https://www.khanacademy.org/

Khan Academy is a free website that contains math, science, and social emotional learning lessons and videos. As our children were growing up, we used the math videos to supplement what they were learning in school. If homework was confusing, we would turn to Khan Academy to explain it to us. Their videos offer child friendly and straightforward instruction. You can search for lessons by age, grade, and subject. Navigating their website is super easy and your kids will enjoy the videos.

I WANT TO REMEMBER:

_____
_____
_____
_____
_____
_____
_____
_____

TECHNOLOGY RULES AT OUR HOUSE:

_____
_____
_____
_____
_____
_____
_____
_____

WEBSITES OR APPS TO CHECK OUT:

_____
_____
_____
_____
_____
_____
_____
_____

TECHNOLOGY-UGH

CHAPTER 2

TECHNOLOGY-UGH

CHAPTER 3

READ, READ, READ, AND READ SOME MORE

There is no such thing as reading too much with your child. Whether it be reading to your child or listening to your child read. Yes, you will need some patience when they ask you to read a book for the fifty-third time. But trust me, these repeated readings are building confidence, vocabulary, and most importantly a love of reading.

There are several books from when our children were growing up that I can recite without skipping a beat. Some of our all-time favorites:

Goodnight Moon (Margaret Wise Brown)

Brown Bear Brown Bear What do you See?
(Bill Martin Jr. and Eric Carle)

The Monster at the End of this Book (Jon Stone)

Gingerbread Baby (Jan Brett)

Blue Hat, Green Hat (Sandra Boynton)

The book, *Gingerbread Baby*, is especially near and dear to our hearts because we have a family tradition of making gingerbread houses. Each December we make gingerbread dough, roll and cut squares, and finally assemble edible houses. We use royal icing and candy to decorate the houses. We store them in bags and snack on them all of December. How does this tradition relate to cultivating a love of reading? When we make the dough, our children are reading a recipe. When we invite others over to decorate a house, our children write the invitations. Decorating gingerbread houses spark their creativity which may lead to other creative actions. And lastly, our gingerbread tradition now includes reading every fiction and nonfiction book about gingerbread that we can find. Reach out to me if you'd like the recipe! melanie.eskildsen.author@gmail.com

CONFIDENCE

Confidence is having a strong feeling about an ability or skill. Often young readers lack confidence. When confidence is lacking, we feel defeated and not good enough.

When I was teaching middle school and high school reading this is how my students started the year with me, lacking confidence. They had teachers who didn't understand that individual students have different reading needs. They may have come from homes where reading was not viewed as a priority. But mostly they needed a boost of confidence. I did this by giving constant encouragement and positive feedback. I had difficult but loving conversations with them. My classroom shelved a vast variety of books whether it be by reading level or topic. And the students got to choose what they read. By giving them choice, encouragement, and confidence they all grew into proficient readers.

Katie was a student from middle school that I will always remember. Katie had been in and out of reading class over the years. She was placed with me in sixth grade to start middle school. Katie was quiet but opinionated. She was diligent in practicing reading daily. Suddenly one day reading made sense to her. I was witness to her lightbulb moment. She walked into my classroom and said, "Mrs. Eskildsen, I get reading. You always tell me to read books that are in my reading level. And I finally understand why!" I asked her to tell me more, an open-ended phrase I often use with students to get them talking. "I was reading a book last night and I could actually answer the questions that went with it. And I liked the book!" Our conversation continued for a while. Finally, Katie said, "I want to tell the principals and everyone else how you helped me to be able to read." Together Katie and I worked on a presentation for the school board of education and administration. On a rainy night in March, Katie and I stood before the school board as she explained how she learned to read and how the reading program helped her. Watching this student who struggled to advocate for herself was an amazing moment in my teaching career.

Katie said what helped her the most was reading books within her reading level. So let's take a minute and explore that idea. When I was teaching middle school and high school reading students were able to choose their own book for independent reading. Students were expected to follow some guidelines for this independent reading. Three times a year students took a test that assigned a reading level, or range of reading level. This reading level was in the form of a number range. For independent reading, they were to choose a book within their range. I believe students can grow and strengthen their reading skills when reading in their range. It is possible that some disagree with me. However, the proof was in the students. Year after year my middle school and high school students improved in their ability to read, write, and comprehend.

VOCABULARY

Vocabulary words are words individuals have in their knowledge bank. They are words a person can easily use and understand what they mean. When children have a wide array of vocabulary words, they are able to communicate better and relate to what they are reading. Having an internal word bank in our brains helps us to communicate effectively. Comprehension is the ability to understand what is being said or read. Again, having a large vocabulary aids in comprehension, the ability to understand what you are reading.

For example, if I grew up fishing with my family, I would have knowledge and vocabulary words related to fishing. When asked to read a book about fishing later on in school, I will have an easier time comprehending and relating to the text based on my experiences. Read more in Chapter 4 about experiences, background knowledge, and vocabulary.

LOVE OF READING

When our oldest daughter started kindergarten, we knew she would be taking a cold lunch daily. On her very first day I put a small piece of paper in her lunch box with a red heart sticker and signed it Love u, Mom. This started a long tradition of writing lunch notes to all three kids. It was fun to hear about her day and the giggles the notes inspired. The lunch room staff enjoyed my notes too! The kind of note I sent eventually evolved into words she could read, maybe the sight words of the week in kindergarten. As they grew older lunch notes contained encouragement or reminders about appointments.

Making your own lunch notes is simple to do. Buy a small notepad and prepare the notes ahead of time by drawing on them or decorating with stickers. You could also use paper you already have at home and cut it into smaller pieces. Leave the paper on the kitchen counter or in a drawer so they are within reach. I had a container sitting on the counter ready with lunch notes, special napkins, and special desserts.

The notes I wrote were relevant to what was happening at home or at school. Sometimes notes included jokes related to an upcoming holiday. These lunch notes encouraged communication, gave our children a purpose for reading, and were fun. Give it a try!

Another important piece of our family's love of reading is our public library. Our public library has an amazing collection of books, magazines, audio books, movies, and games for small children. There is a small play area where kids are encouraged to play, make noise, and be creative. They offer story time for infants and preschool age children. There are often programs like meeting an author or reading a therapy dog. The summer reading program keeps them engaged with books and learning all summer long. By early middle school our children were volunteering at the public library. They would lead art activities for younger students or help the library staff prepare and clean-up activities. Their volunteer time was an enriching opportunity to give back to the library that had done so much for them.

Who or what influenced you to read? When I think back to my childhood about who influenced me as a reader, two important women come to mind: Grandma June and Mrs.

Shane. Grandma June was the only living grandparent I had growing up, while Mrs. Shane was my fourth-grade teacher. Both of these women were critical to me growing up as a reader.

Grandma June was a sweet, honest, and loving grandma. Seems to me she was either reading or in the kitchen. When I spent time at her house, I was either reading or in the kitchen helping. She had a stack of books for when her grandchildren visited. Now these books never seemed to change but I didn't mind. Rereading has its benefits too. She also enjoyed taking me to the public library. She would be upstairs, and I would race downstairs to the children's department. As she aged, it was me taking her to the library to check out books. She continued to read into her ninety's. After her passing, our family gifted large print books to our public library. A lasting legacy for a grandma who loved reading.

While our children were growing up Grandma June lived in an assisted living facility. We would visit her every Sunday. I would pack a large bag of toys and books to take along. Grandma was always excited to see what books the kids were reading. I'll always remember the Halloween she read *Ten Timid Ghosts* by Jennifer O'Connell to our kids. Grandma found pure joy in each page. The pictures made her laugh. The rhyme and repetition in the book rolled off her tongue with grace. Even though this was at least fifteen years ago I remember it like it was yesterday. Books have the potential for lasting memories when shared with loved ones.

Another influence in my reading life was Mrs. Shane, my 4th grade teacher. What set Mrs. Shane apart was suddenly reading and language was an interesting thing to do. She taught us sign language, enough to sign songs and recite poetry by signing. Her classroom made reading a priority. Books and magazines of all kinds were everywhere. The reading corner was lined with fluffy pillows and a clawfoot bathtub. Reading in that tub was the place to be! She also read aloud to us in a dramatic and engaging way. She introduced me to new authors like Beverly Cleary, Judy Blume, and Laura Ingalls Wilder. Mrs. Shane is still an integral part of my life. We communicate almost daily about life, parenting, and teaching. Her influence is woven deeply into who I am as a mom, wife, and teacher.

READING ROUTINES

Routines are patterns in behavior that develop over time. The way I prepare for a school day is a routine: let the dog out, shower, eat breakfast, and make lunch. If this sequence is done in a different order my whole day is off. Are you like that?

Take advantage of bedtime to create reading routines. Children thrive on routines. They tend to behave better when they know what is going to happen or know what is expected of them.

As our children were growing up, we had a bedtime routine: get pajamas on, brush teeth, read aloud at least one book, read quietly in their bed, then finally lights out. Adding reading to our bedtime routine created a time to enjoy books at a set time each day. Reading aloud each day builds vocabulary, knowledge about their world, and adds pleasure to the day.

While growing up our children had book boxes at the foot of their bed. These were wooden boxes that measured about 8" x 12". The boxes did not have a cover, so it was more like a wooden basket. They were able to keep between ten and fifteen books in their boxes. Our children picked books from our shelf or the public library to go in their book boxes. I had fun sneaking in holiday books or joke books. Never underestimate changing things up a little. Kids notice and it increases their enjoyment and engagement in reading.

NURSERY RHYMES

Nursery rhymes are a fun way to build vocabulary, practice rhyming, and build a connection with your child. Nursery rhymes are simply fun too. Make up some actions with your hands or dance around as you say the nursery rhyme. Building vocabulary will help your child as they learn to read. When they encounter a word, they may be able to relate back to the nursery rhyme to pronounce or understand the meaning of the word. Learning to rhyme is an important milestone when learning to read. When children rhyme, they are manipulating sounds which is what they do as readers. Lastly, reciting nursery rhymes with your child is a time when you can build a connection, or bonding time.

As a family we incorporated nursery rhymes when the moment seemed right. Nursery rhymes can be recited during everyday activities like while waiting in line at a grocery store or waiting for a doctor appointment. When our kids were babies, diaper changing time was my favorite time to incorporate nursery rhymes. It distracted me from the task at hand and they had no choice but to engage in the rhyming. These were some of our favorite nursery rhymes.

One, two, buckle my shoe
Three, four, shut the door
Five, six, pick up sticks
Seven, eight, lay them straight
Nine, ten, a big fat hen

The itsy, bitsy spider went up the water spout,
Down came the rain and washed the spider out.
Out came the sun and dried up all the rain,
And the itsy, bitsy spider went up the spout again.

Star light, star bright
First star I see tonight.
I wish I may, I wish I might
Have the wish I wish tonight.

Our children enjoy quiet reading time together, ages 3 and 1.

BASIC SKILLS

Until now this chapter has focused on reading to your child. When your child enters school, they will begin to learn to read on their own. Reading aloud, sharing experiences, teaching vocabulary words will all help them as they learn to read.

When it comes to teaching young children to read, I believe there are some basic skills they need to acquire. These basic skills are listed below.

- How to hold a book correctly to be able to read
- Books move from left to right, sentences move from left to right, individual words move from left to right
- Memorize sight words
- Some words can be read by sounding them out
- Use pictures and context for clues to read unknown words and comprehend the story
- Imagine in your head what is happening in the book

HOLDING A BOOK

You probably don't pay attention to how you hold a book. We learn by others modeling that books are held right side up. I suggest you model this for children and call it like it is. "I am holding the book this way so the words and pictures are not upside down." or "When I read this is how I hold the book."

MOVING FROM LEFT TO RIGHT

As children grow, they will learn more about the words left and right and their meaning. Young children can however learn about directionality with books through modeling. Try saying to your child, "I turn the page this way to read what happens next" or "I start reading here and then move this way" (pointing left to right).

TIME TO MEMORIZE SIGHT WORDS

Similar to math facts, some words just have to be memorized. It's just the way it is. Some words have unusual vowel patterns or letter combinations that do not follow common rules. When your child is ready, start helping them memorize sight words. In our family it was when our children started kindergarten. We received a list from the teacher to guide our at-home practice. Ask your child's teacher for a list of sight words you can practice at home.

I've included a common word list that I've seen used in various school districts. It's called the Dolch Word List. You'll notice the complexity of words increases as children increase in age. When I introduce these words to children, I start with three. Just three to start. Pick three and work with them like crazy. When it seems those three words are mastered, add three more. There is no scientific research behind choosing three words, it is what has worked for me over the years. If your child is having an easy time memorizing three, add a couple more words. If your child is really struggling remembering words, take a break for a couple weeks and then come back to it. They may not be ready yet.

All 220 Dolch words by grade in alphabetical order

Pre-Primer		Primer		First Grade		Second Grade		Third Grade	
a	look	all	out	after	let	always	or	about	laugh
and	make	am	please	again	live	around	pull	better	light
away	me	are	pretty	an	may	because	read	bring	long
big	my	at	ran	any	of	been	right	carry	much
blue	not	ate	ride	as	old	before	sing	clean	myself
can	one	be	saw	ask	once	best	sit	cut	never
come	play	black	say	by	open	both	sleep	done	only
down	red	brown	she	could	over	buy	tell	draw	own
find	run	but	so	every	put	call	their	drink	pick
for	said	came	soon	fly	round	cold	these	eight	seven
funny	see	did	that	from	some	does	those	fall	shall
go	the	do	there	give	stop	don't	upon	far	show
help	three	eat	they	going	take	fast	us	full	six
here	to	four	this	had	thank	first	use	got	small
I	two	get	too	has	them	five	very	grow	start
in	up	good	under	her	then	found	wash	hold	ten
is	we	have	want	him	think	gave	which	hot	today
it	where	he	was	his	walk	goes	why	hurt	together
jump	yellow	into	well	how	were	green	wish	if	try
little	you	like	went	just	when	its	work	keep	warm
		must	what	know		made	would	kind	
		new	white			many	write		
		no	who			off	your		
		now	will						
		on	with						
		our	yes						

www.dolchword.net

Practicing sight words by writing them in the sand.

Some of my favorite ways to practice sight words are messy and fun. Give it a try!

- Make a box of instant pudding. Put a small amount of pudding on a cookie sheet. Encourage your child to use their fingers to write sight words in the pudding.
- Use letter magnets to make words
- Use modeling dough to make words
- Write words on sticky paper. Hide the words around the house. Have your child find them and read them.

Homemade modeling Dough

What you'll need:
1 cup all-purpose flour
1 cup water
2 teaspoons cream of tartar
⅓ cup salt
1 tablespoon vegetable oil
Food coloring

How to make:

Stir together the above ingredients in a two-quart saucepan.

Cook over low/medium heat, stirring the entire time.

Continue stirring until the mixture is thickened and begins to form a ball.

Remove dough from pan. Place on a plate to cool.

I WANT TO REMEMBER:

_____
_____
_____
_____
_____
_____
_____
_____
_____

DAILY ROUTINES AND HOW TO ADD READING:

_____
_____
_____
_____
_____
_____
_____
_____
_____

MY CHILD WOULD ENJOY PRACTICING SIGHT WORDS BY:

_____
_____
_____
_____
_____
_____
_____

READ, READ, READ, AND READ SOME MORE

CHAPTER 3

READ, READ, READ, AND READ SOME MORE

CHAPTER 4

EXPERIENCES TO BUILD BACKGROUND KNOWLEDGE

B ack in Chapter 1, I introduced you to my simple belief: embrace everyday life as a teachable moment. Over time, those moments culminate into children who love learning, reading, and writing. Let's put that into practice!

Experiencing a new concept, activity, or experience with our children is probably our favorite part of parenting! These experiences help to raise a child who loves reading and learning. You know the look, wide eyed and full of questions. Oh, how I love that look on a child's face! How lucky are we to be the ones to help them learn, develop, and grow. It is a responsibility I do not take lightly.

In the summer of 2013, we traveled with grandparents to Washington, D.C. to visit family. This trip was rich with experiences for our children! We visited the Ford's Theatre where Abraham Lincoln was shot. We toured all the monuments in Washington D.C. We visited museums and learned about U.S. and aviation history. We walked through George Washington's house. Our kids heard first hand stories from their grandpa about the Vietnam War. These experiences gave our children new vocabulary, knowledge, and experiences to draw from later in life.

WHAT IS BACKGROUND KNOWLEDGE?

Different experiences with your child lead to background knowledge. Having knowledge and vocabulary about a subject is background knowledge. For example, our children grew up planting, tending to, harvesting, and preserving food from our garden. Their experiences with gardening widened their understanding and vocabulary related to gardening.

Comprehending is being able to retell a story with details and answer questions about it. Comprehension goes a bit deeper by children being able to explain a character's feelings or actions and use their own knowledge to predict and understand hidden meanings in a story. Again, experiences provide the background knowledge your child needs to read and clearly comprehend a story.

It seems every year my students read a book about the post office and mail system. I further the learning and experience by teaching them how to write a letter and address an envelope. Then we take a quick walk to the post office and mail it. When their letters arrive at their house, they bring them to school, and we continue the conversation. What they just read in a book has come to life. They are doing what they read about. This experience with sending mail brings the book to life. It gives them the experience to better understand where mail comes from and how it gets from place to place.

EVERYDAY EXPERIENCES

The year I began teaching was overwhelming and exciting all at the same time. It was exciting because what I had worked so hard for in college was happening, a kindergarten classroom of my very own. It was overwhelming because my position was new, which meant a new classroom and very few supplies. I remember it hitting me about 2 months into the new school year: this overwhelmed feeling. After the students had left for the day, I stood in my classroom looking around and crying. My students did not have the ideal classroom for which I had hoped. The play areas were quite bare. I visited many thrift stores trying to find bits and pieces of educational toys I could afford. While I stood in my classroom crying a newly retired kindergarten teacher stopped in. She was highly regarded in the district and had returned to help with substitute teaching. She was a kind sweet woman. She got close to me, held my hand and said, "Melanie, these children do not need things, they need YOU. They need you to teach them, guide them, and create experiences for them. Things don't matter, it's YOU they need." Her words left a lasting impression on me. You are that for your child. You provide experiences for them to grow and learn. What you do for your child and with your child matters.

LEAN ON FRIENDS AND FAMILY

You are not the only important person in your child's life that can give them experiences. Take a minute and think about those close to you who might have special skills, hobbies, or jobs. Maybe it's friends, colleagues, family members, or other parents. What could they teach your child? What new experience could they share? Is there something your child is interested in learning more about?

In our family it's Grandma and Grandpa Eskildsen. Growing up our children would spend about three weekends a year with them. During their time away they would learn about sewing, quilting, baking, cooking, and woodworking. I'll always remember the weekend they each came home with handmade gifts for me. The pride and joy on their faces is forever etched in my memory. Katherine made me banana muffins and painted a wooden welcome sign. She sketched out the design of the sign. Grandpa helped her hammer the wood together and then she painted a beautiful daisy on it. Seth made two wooden birds for me to decorate with outside. He searched through bird books to find just the right type of birds I'd like: a woodpecker and a chickadee. He said the chickadee would always remind me of him. That kid wholeheartedly believed the chickadees would talk back to him. And our youngest, Olivia, came home with two pillows she made. One for dad and one for me. She decided on the fabric and did the sewing herself. Those crafts they made still adorn our house today. And those experiences left a lasting impression on our children.

Every day we have an opportunity to share a new experience or activity with a child. This list includes favorites from our family.

Experiences that promote reading skills:

- Participating in story time at the public library
- Checking out books, magazines, toys, audio books from the public library
- Write a thank you card for a gift that was received
- Trying new activities and sports
- Discover ways to volunteer in your community
- Write a letter to a relative asking to purchase from a fundraising event

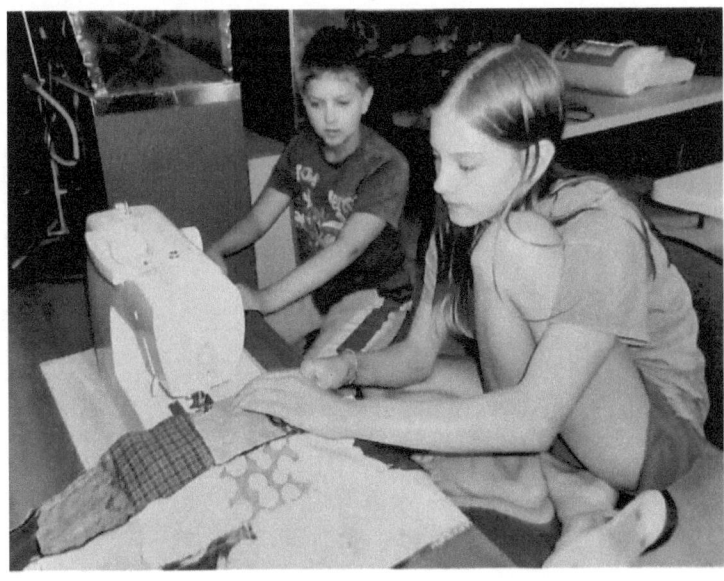

Learning to sew with Grandma Eskildsen

Woodworking with Grandpa Eskildsen

Visiting a farm and trying horseback riding, age 4.

Katherine and Grandpa Eskildsen using a scroll saw

*Learning to peel corn on the cob. So many new words to
learn: cob, kernel, silk, ear of corn, stalk, sticky.*

Visiting our friend the firefighter

Visiting the Laura Ingalls Wilder home and museum.

I WANT TO REMEMBER:

_____
_____
_____
_____
_____
_____
_____
_____
_____

MY CHILD IS INTERESTED IN LEARNING ABOUT:

_____
_____
_____
_____
_____
_____
_____
_____
_____

WHO CAN I LEAN ON:

_____
_____
_____
_____
_____
_____
_____
_____

CHAPTER 5

KEEP IT GOING!

CHAPTER 5

KEEP IT GOING!

Up until now, you've read stories and ideas to help your child grow up in a literacy rich environment. Literacy is the ability to read and write. So, a literacy rich environment is one where reading and writing is valued and practiced. How do we keep children interested in reading and learning so they keep coming back for more? What can you do to guide them to choose reading over a different activity?

In this chapter we'll explore reading momentum, the reading and writing connection, and various ways to keep kids interested in reading. In no time you will be raising a reader!

READING MOMENTUM

When I think about keeping reading going, I think of reading momentum. I like to use this wording with my students because momentum means to keep going. When I first start working with students, I talk to them about staying focused on their reading. Can you stay focused on reading for two minutes? After several weeks, can you stay focused on reading for four minutes? By doing this we are gradually helping children build and maintain reading momentum or stamina. Now I don't sit next to a child with a timer and time their reading. But helping them build their reading stamina is an important step in the learning to read process.

Besides reading, we can keep the momentum or excitement going about reading and books. To keep up the reading momentum I like to allow students to freely choose what they read. Think about how little children are in control of their world. Allowing them the freedom to choose books gives them ownership to their reading. At home and school, I like to frequently change books around. When our children were younger books sometimes went missing. And by missing, I mean they went in a tote in the closet. After a few weeks, I would bring those books out again. When those books reappeared, they were like new. By the way, I did this with toys too as our children were growing. Changing up books along with toys creates a newness or novelty to the toy or book.

THE READING AND WRITING CONNECTION

There is no doubt reading and writing are connected or better yet intertwined. If you can read it, the chances are good you can write it. Likewise, what you can write you can read. So how do we help children make the connection? When reading with students I often say things like, "What is coming out of my mouth matches the words on the page." Or "Make it match." Sometimes I'll record students reading a familiar story. Then we listen to the recording and see if what they say matches the words on the page.

When writing I'll often ask students what they want to write so they can say it first. Then we write one word at a time. Sometimes they sound out words to write. Other times they have the word memorized to write it; this goes back to the list of sight words shared in chapter three.

WAYS TO KEEP THEM INTERESTED

Over the years we've found different ways to keep our kids interested in reading. We sought out books that were interesting to our children. When they were old enough, they volunteered at our public library. On family trips to a new city, we would find books related to the trip. Traveling was a great time to incorporate geography books too. Travel journals were also a big part of our road trips and vacations. Sometimes we used notebooks and sometimes I made travel journals with white printer paper. Our children were encouraged to write and draw about our daily family adventures. It is fun to look back at their travel journals now.

As a family we listen to audio books. We listened to picture books when they were little and gradually graduated to chapter books. Choosing an audio book that is a series encouraged our children to read the next book in the series. Our favorite series is Masterminds by Gordon Korman. His books appeal to children and adults alike.

As *Raising Readers* comes to a close, I encourage you to reflect on my belief: embrace everyday life as a teachable moment. Over time, those moments culminate into children who love learning, reading, and writing. What can you do today to raise a reader?

I WANT TO REMEMBER:

_____
_____
_____
_____
_____
_____
_____
_____

HOW CAN I KEEP MY CHILD INTERESTED IN READING:

_____
_____
_____
_____
_____
_____
_____
_____

WAYS TO INCORPORATE DAILY READING AND WRITING OPPORTUNITIES:

_____
_____
_____
_____
_____
_____
_____

KEEP IT GOING!

CHAPTER 5

CHAPTER 5

KEEP IT GOING!

CHAPTER 5

KEEP IT GOING!

www.ingramcontent.com/pod-product-compliance
Lightning Source LLC
Chambersburg PA
CBHW030512130626
46549CB00007B/2956